Pragmatic Wisdom Vol. 2

Stoic Lessons on Avoiding the Public Eye

James Bellerjeau

A Fine Idea

Copyright © 2025 by James Bellerjeau

All rights reserved.

No portion of this book may be reproduced in any form without written permission from the publisher or author, except as permitted by U.S. copyright law.

Contents

1. Why Do Anything? An Introduction to the Stoic Lessons ... 1
2. On Consuming Social Media ... 3
3. On Friends, Not Followers ... 7
4. On Public Opinion ... 9
5. On Attending to Yourself ... 13
6. On Introverts ... 17
7. On Keeping a Low Profile ... 21
8. On Looking Within ... 27
9. On Word Games and Worthy Matters ... 31
10. On Those Who Will Not See ... 35
11. On Seven Popular Places ... 41
12. On Philosophers, New and Old ... 47
13. On Abiding in One Place ... 51
14. On Mind Viruses ... 57
15. On Popular Authors ... 63

16.	On the Greatest Threat	69
17.	On Treading Safely	73
18.	On Slogans	79
19.	On Being a Nonconformist	87

Chapter One

Why Do Anything? An Introduction to the Stoic Lessons

Dear friends. Join me on a journey to discover what it means to live a good life. Our inspiration in this quest is Seneca's Moral Letters to Lucilius, revisited and revised for our modern times. The search for what it means to live a good life was not new in Seneca's day, and it will not be old when we are all long gone.

Although these are not Seneca's letters, they honor both his wisdom and his instructions for new students. That is, we should grapple with deep thoughts and make our understanding of the truth personal.

Because no one has a monopoly on the truth, we can each contribute to the puzzle. **The reason to do anything is to answer a question that has not been answered, or at a minimum to answer it for yourself.**

In answering life's deepest questions, would it not be foolish for us to pass by the foundational stones laid by the great thinkers who labored before us? Seneca himself in search of inspiration says in his Letter 2:

> I am wont to cross over even into the enemy's camp, — not as a deserter, but as a scout.

Let us all be avid scouts of the great thinkers, seeking out their every camp with the mindset of anthropologists unearthing meaning from among the ruins. Although Seneca's words have been mined by many for centuries, each generation keeps turning up gemstones.

Thus, with this series of Pragmatic Wisdom for Busy People, let us polish old stones to show them in a new light, and in washing off the mud and debris, reveal what fresh reflections may appear.

Be well.

PS — You can read each of the volumes independently, as it suits your time and your interests. Dedicated readers will find, however, that their understanding of each volume will increase upon reading further volumes. The sincere student may therefore wish to have the full set of Stoic letters: Pragmatic Wisdom for the Sincere Student.

Chapter Two

On Consuming Social Media

A steady diet of social media will leave you bloated but undernourished

Greetings dear reader!

Judging by your latest message to me, I am positively inclined about your prospects. You do not flit from topic to topic or overly engage yourself with the latest story to trend.

The frantic hunt for likes and retweets is a sign of a distracted mind. The truest measure of a well-focused person is the extent to which they can leave aside the passions of the day in favor of the priorities they previously set.

A steady diet of social media will leave you bloated but undernourished. You will grow fat with trivialities as quickly as you grow unhealthy in your thinking.

In contrast, the proudest result of deep thought is a truth that you can express in a few words. Even though it may be devoured in a single bite, the healthy nugget of truth will nourish the wise. It is possible, but unlikely, to find deep truth in social media; remember most miners will go bankrupt.

Your challenge in separating the wheat from the chaff grows daily. The sheer volume of voices crying out to be heard threatens to deafen even the most astute listener.

Your chances of finding useful content today are like plucking up a handful of sand and expecting to sift out a diamond ring. You might bulldoze the entire beach and end up with nothing but silica for your efforts, not to mention a large bill for diesel.

What is a hungry consumer of a sensitive disposition to do? Rather than sample a thousand dishes in the hope of finding one that is not poisoned, better engage the services of a seasoned taster.

Find a Sherpa to lead you up the mountain, and to shoulder the bigger part of the load while they're at it. Unlike the mission facing the crew of the Starship Enterprise, this territory has been explored and mapped and its secrets laid bare.

Your challenge then is not to walk every inch of the land yourself, but to leverage the mapmakers' toil. Concretely, I tell you this: Select no more than five trackers whose navigation skills you trust. What lights guide their sojourns in the wilderness of the web? The best of them will give up their secrets willingly, for they want other pilgrims to join them on the path.

What compass guides my step, you ask? Honestly, ask first if you should step out your door at all. Consider whether you need to depart your oasis, for the desert is deep and wide and unforgiving.

ON CONSUMING SOCIAL MEDIA

The greater portion of what mankind has learned was uncovered long ago, and the sands of time have not buried it yet. Seneca, Marcus Aurelius, and Epictetus are some of the best guides you will find in any age.

But if you are compelled to seek out fresher fare, try the Farnam Street blog, and the Almanack of Naval Rivikant. These alone are deep enough wells from which to drink richly whenever thirst comes upon you.

Enduring truths are available freely to all. I would anyway urge caution when dealing with truthtellers who seek compensation for their wisdom. By selling their wares, they must give thought to their attractive presentation.

A lasting truth cannot be possessed, only uncovered, and once uncovered is made greater by sharing.

The wise profit from sharing their thoughts, not from selling them.

Be well.

Chapter Three

On Friends, Not Followers

A true friend will tell you when you are being a fool

Greetings dear reader!

You ask whether to congratulate the latest pop star to attract one hundred million followers on social media. Rather offer your condolences to Justin Bieber than your praise.

Followers want nothing more than to consume you, while a friend wants to see you nourished. Do not celebrate another cannibal joining the banquet when you are the main dish.

"But," you say, "am I not made greater by the acclamation of the masses?" If wisdom is rare in individuals, even fainter is your chance of finding it among the multitude.

This is because the masses are but one step removed from the mob, and the mob knows no morals. The mob knows only that it must do more of whatever it is doing at that moment.

Better a single voice speaking reason, thereby calming the passions of the throng, than a stadium of spectators cheering the games along.

"But my post was upvoted a hundred times and shared by two hundred more!" I hear you already. "Surely that demonstrates the truth of what I say."

I tell you, look at our politicians raining cash down upon a welcoming public. Should Congress take comfort in the wisdom of its course because polls show a majority approve?

Say you offer guests at your next dinner party the boon of carrying away the silver plates. Surely a supermajority of them will upvote your largesse. Now just imagine schoolchildren's universal chorus of likes when you declare candy for lunch and homework is forbidden.

The only thing such numbers tell us is that a great number of people can be greatly wrong about a great many things.

A true friend will tell you when you are being a fool. A true friend will risk your ire by not praising that, which is not praiseworthy.

You do not need a thousand to point out your flaws. A single friend will do, if they truly know you and if you listen truly.

And better the heartfelt praise of a single one who knows you, than the thunderous applause of thousands who are blind.

Be well.

Chapter Four

On Public Opinion

Nothing is more dangerous to your reputation than exposure to public view in the circus of social media

Greetings dear reader!

Do you ask me what you should avoid above all else? Public opinion, I say; for as yet none have managed to navigate it without peril. And no one ever ventured forth into the public arena without being tainted by what they encountered there.

When you swim in sewage you can't help but come away smelling sour. To court public attention is to court disaster because there is no chance that you will not be confronted with the basest and vilest among us. The more you seek to spread your reach, the greater your risk of getting your fingers smacked.

Nothing is more dangerous to your reputation than exposure to public view in the circus of social media. By crying out in this arena, you draw the attention of the mob that has no interest in building you up, but only in tearing you down.

It matters not what you say or mean; it only matters how what you say can be misunderstood. We are challenged enough to make our point clear in a debate with equally armed combatants, where there are no limits on our time to speak, and our opponent is primed to listen. Even here, a meeting of the minds is the rare outcome of hard-fought sparring.

What chance, then, can you hope to have in the social media sphere, where every tongue is sharpened, and your words are deliberately twisted in knots to tie you to positions you do not hold?

- "Can you believe how bigoted he is," the crowd bays.
- "He offended me," wails another.
- "I am offended on behalf of another!"

That you have committed no actual harm is irrelevant, and there need be no sin. When the crowd's bloodlust is aroused and the tweets are flying, the question is never whether there will be a cancellation, only whose turn it is in the dock today.

And don't think you can throw yourself upon the mercy of this court. Mercy only grows in soil watered by compassion and understanding, of which this mob has neither in abundance. The only water flowing on these grounds is the raging flood that etches first channels and then ravines into even the firmest bedrock.

Nay, no matter how abject your apology, absolution will not be forthcoming. Rather, we observe the opposite: the stronger your apology, the graver must have been your offense!

But the greatest harm is to your own soul. By offering an apology where none is due, you give credence to the false claims against you. Do not weaken your conviction by submitting to unjust jabs. Just as the valid argument does not become so by virtue of the multitude's praise, nor does the jabbering of a lunatic horde render your point defective.

"But surely it is worthwhile to put down enduring truths. For even though many will misunderstand, and even more will not hear, still the benefit will be real to some." True enough, dear reader.

If you do expose your thoughts to public opinion for this noble purpose, make sure that you have first built up your defenses as carefully as you have built your arguments.

Until you are ready, it is safest to withdraw into solitude and contemplation. In the quiet, your mind can expand and roam. Spend your time with a small group of friends, who are equally committed to self-improvement.

These friends will identify the flaws in your ill-considered arguments, but will not declare *you* flawed as a result. Your own thoughts are improved by refining away these flaws, and thus the battle leaves you strengthened rather than worn.

Lest you think that I write for my own sake alone, I shall share with you three excellent sayings along the same lines. Consider the first in payment of my debt to you and the others as advance deposits.

Epictetus serves up this reminder that the persons we surround ourselves with are vital to our progress:

> The key is to keep company only with people who uplift you, whose presence calls forth your best.

You might think it was his great wealth and power that led Bernard Baruch to this next thought, but the wisdom in it is equally available to the pauper:

> Be who you are and say what you feel, because those who mind don't matter, and those who matter don't mind.

And the third saying, from modern-day philosopher Henry David Thoreau, reminds us that we need nothing so much as our own well-ordered mind:

> I never found the companion that was so companionable as solitude. We are for the most part more lonely when we go abroad among men than when we stay in our chambers.

Take these words to heart, dear reader, to fortify your resolve neither to be shaken by praise nor blame.

True goodness comes from within, and thus your focus lies there.

Be well.

Chapter Five

On Attending to Yourself

There is no one with whom you more profitably spend time than yourself

I mean what I say: You should scorn public opinion, shun social media, and be shaken neither by praise nor blame.

Do not trust a thoughtless person. Leave them all if you can but trust yourself.

Build a foundation within yourself and it cannot be eroded by what others say or do. If you rely for your strength on others, it may be taken away at any time.

As the Buddhist scriptures enshrined in the Dhammapada urge us:

> Better than a hundred years not considering how all things arise and pass away is one single day of

life if one considers how all things arise and pass
away.

When you are true to yourself, you need not fear the judgment of time. Though your fellow man may judge you, aroused by anonymity, anger, and spite, you can rest assured that you are true to a higher purpose. Better solitary confinement to preserve your peace of mind!

Here is how I wish to see you. No, rather what I already see, for a wish is an empty thought: there is no one with whom you more profitably spend time than yourself.

You are already showing your understanding and strength of character by confidently putting our lessons into practice. Many hear, but few listen. I rejoice that your ears are open, and wise words are falling on the fertile ground of your mind.

A sound mind is a foundation that can support the grandest structures. Continue on in this way, and nothing will slow your progress.

As is now my habit, I send you along your way with a token. It is another true wisdom from the mind of Henry David Thoreau:

> What you get by achieving your goals is not as important as what you become by achieving your goals.

The masses foolishly mistake the goalpost for the goal. They spend their mortal lives on the idea that accomplishment is measured in things.

You, however, will appreciate that real wisdom comes in understanding that it is the daily shaping, turning, and grinding of the stone on the wheel that makes the gem, and not the shiny bauble that any fool can simply buy.

Be well.

Chapter Six

On Introverts

Introversion is not something that is remedied by exposure. If anything, repeated forays out of comfortable seclusion only strengthen the desire to return to safety

I talked recently with your friend D. after a lecture. He is capable and gives the impression immediately that he is a sincere student.

When I challenged him, he was at first hesitant to respond. I could see him drawing away before he pulled himself back, and I fault him not. It is a natural instinct, particularly among the inexperienced, to avoid a confrontation and retreat to safety.

An introvert is never so safe as inside their own head.

And I do not doubt that though he will be cured of the affliction of youth, he will continue to shy away even as his experience grows.

Introversion is not something that is remedied by exposure. If anything, repeated forays out of comfortable seclusion only strengthen the desire to return to safety.

Examples of accomplished recluses come easily to mind: Howard Hughes was fantastically wealthy and freakishly eccentric, all but guaranteeing he would be of constant interest.

He could so little bear interaction with others that he would shut himself away; he spent four months in a studio screening room without once leaving. Upon checking in to the Desert Inn in Las Vegas, he refused to leave, eventually buying the hotel to avoid confronting the owners.

Or consider Harper Lee, who blazed into the public eye after publishing *To Kill a Mockingbird*. We could not get enough of her, but she had her fill of us and so retreated into isolation and published nothing more for over half a century.

Some types of people thrive on exposure, while others wilt and withdraw.

As I noted, practice alone cannot undo the introvert element of human nature. If we could simply wish to change our nature and make it so, wishes would rule the world.

An introvert by birth will be an introvert at death, no matter how often they force themselves into public interactions to lessen the power of their feelings.

But you need not worry if you yourself or another you encounter has introvert tendencies because all that your progress requires is within you.

It is time now for my parting remark. Listen and learn from this lovely lesson:

ON INTROVERTS

> When witnessing the good action of another, encourage yourself to follow his example. Hearing of the mistaken action of another, advise yourself not to emulate it. Censure yourself, never another.

This dear reader is the wisdom of the Zen practitioners, who remind us we can behave correctly when there is no one about to correct us.

The introvert need never be separated from both good and bad examples, and from both, they may take their lessons though they stay secluded.

When we bring to mind a virtuous act, it serves as an example for us to emulate. And observing the foolish in their cavorting, we see clearly the line we know not to cross.

Blessed are they who, by keeping both the worst and best in their thoughts, know which paths to avoid and which to favor.

Though we may shun all others as a measure of our self-sufficiency, we can still measure ourselves against the standards of humankind.

Be well.

Chapter Seven

On Keeping a Low Profile

I say this: The mob will hate you if you are wrong, and they will hate you even more if you are right

It is worthy to cultivate a sound mind in a sound body.

Our peace of mind is threatened most by three types of worry:

- of the many failures that can afflict our bodies,
- that we will lack the things we think we need, and
- what other people think of us.

Of these, the interaction with your fellow man creates the greatest potential for trouble.

All that the hermit lacks in possessions, comfort, and interactions, he gains in being free of the affliction that is neighbors.

In solitude, you can focus on your own thoughts. In a neighborhood you can scarcely be heard among the din of silently competing boasts: The Pelosis installed a $20,000 refrigerator, the Bidens bought a second home, and the Trumps have gilded their very bathrooms.

You are making do with a three-year-old BMW, and your last vacation was to Boston, not the Bahamas. Oh! for the days when you only had to keep up with the Jones.

Just as you cannot help but notice the crazed consumption of your neighbors, never be lulled into thinking your actions are beneath their regard.

And though you feel you must wither under your neighbors' condescension when you are outdone, that is a faint breeze compared to the furies you will unleash if you temporarily pull ahead on the hedonistic treadmill.

Our fellow man hates us least when we know our station, and that is always comfortably below our fellow, wherever the level may be. We can suffer grievous physical injuries and carry on, but an injured pride is fatal to many a friendship.

You cannot hide from prying eyes, short of taking up your own hermit's cave, but you can try not to draw attention, either positive or negative.

Remember, you can be hurt by the one, by the few, or by the many. If you wish not to be mauled, don't stroll through the zoo wafting meat perfume.

Putting a sign on your lawn bearing a political message will draw the ire of different-thinking neighbors like ants to crumbs at a picnic.

ON KEEPING A LOW PROFILE

If you hold opinions that may inflame passions among arsonists, do not blow on them in the hopes of making them grow, because it is you who stands directly in front of the fire. Rather whisper such seditious thoughts to yourself.

"But," you say "do you really counsel letting the ignorant masses stifle free speech and clear thinking? It is the mob who are mistaken, and by remaining silent, do I not enable mindless tyranny?"

I say this: The mob will hate you if you are wrong, and they will hate you even more if you are right.

By speaking out as an individual, you threaten the consensus. Nothing is more harmful to the shallow-minded, because they instinctively grasp that their fragile foundations are built on sand. Thus, they cannot permit a wise voice to even puff in their direction.

By withdrawing from the public eye, you must take care not to present yourself as an easy target. A drop of blood in the water attracts sharks from fathoms away.

So too is a need for affirmation fatal to your safe passage. You withdraw not because you fear the public's opinion, whether good or bad, but because it does not concern you.

What concerns you is your well-ordered mind and your self-possession, and this no mob can plunder. In needing only basics and eschewing luxury, you find sanctuary within your own four walls. You then can busy yourself with the job of clear thinking.

Much like a road needs to be cleared of all obstacles before you can safely navigate it, your mind speeds along that much more expeditiously when cleared of extraneous fears, worries, and wants.

There is one exception to the basic rule of keeping a low profile: When passions are inflamed to such an extent that you may not be silent, lest a negative inference be drawn.

When silence is not an option, neither is meekly submitting to the mob.

Though they would tear you limb from limb, you must not say things you do not believe are true. This will erode your soul, and in short order your body as well, as surely as the mob's pitchforks and torches, but with the difference that you inflict the wound on yourself.

You may know a great truth and keep it to yourself because the mob's ears are shut. Fair enough. But you cannot lend your voice to a mob committing wrong, for this is both to perpetuate the wrong and give the mob power over the one possession that is truly yours, your self-possession.

You eagerly await a final truth that I should now share with you. Such is the quality of this addition to our store of wisdom that we may shout it from the rooftops, hear all who may.

> It is not the man who has too little, but the man who craves more, who is poor.

Here I return to our most trusted of guides, the Stoics, and that towering figure among them, Seneca. It was his particular gift to collect, curate, and sift the wisdom of the ages, and his courage to make it available for all with the desire to know it.

Man is the only animal that can instantly create both scarcity and abundance with the exact same quantity of material.

You are poor when you think you lack something, and you are as rich as your appreciation for what you have.

Be well.

Chapter Eight

On Looking Within

For us to know the true worth of something, we must look beyond the packaging. And this takes time

You are making a sound investment, one which will pay dividends, if you do as you describe in your letters, in regularly training your mind.

There are many before you who will stand as gatekeepers, and not all of them are benevolent:

- from the university administrators who say you cannot be educated without their degree,

- to the licensing bodies who claim you cannot run your business without their certification,

- to the self-help authors who say you cannot be happy without buying their book.

When it comes to achieving a well-ordered mind, none of these are required. They are in fact obstacles to progress, but only for those who listen to them. All you need to advance is within.

Think of the gardener quietly tilling the soil, patiently weeding, and enjoying the feel of the sun on her face as she watches her seedlings sprout and grow. It was no diploma or license that enabled this wholesome and satisfying work.

The poet putting pen to paper is tapping into a spring that flows purest when it is free of external pollution. The self-help book might as well be called the self-doubt book for all the good it will do someone who is trying to master their thoughts and emotions.

We are easily fooled by outward appearances because we are encouraged to be productive.

"What do you mean?" you say, "Is it not correct to be about our business in an efficient way? What harm is there in productivity?"

I will tell you, dear reader, where the harm lies. When you have set your goals around productivity, you are enabling yourself to do more. The more you can do, the more you agree to do, and the more productive you become. Except in your headlong rush, you have learned that you must make quick decisions, and hence you look no further than the surface of things.

- "This one has many followers and is popular on the talk shows. I will listen to him because he must have something important to say."

- "That one has accumulated great wealth and has three companies. I will work with her because she must be a brilliant businessperson."

- "This book is a New York Times bestseller. I will read it because it must contain important truths."

ON LOOKING WITHIN

Can you ever be wrong in following the masses? Going along with the crowd brings you certainty, yes, but it is comfort only that you will not be alone in your beliefs, not that they are necessarily true.

For does not the crowd celebrate a person for their designer clothes, their sports car, and their expensive watch? When this tells you almost nothing about the person inside those clothes and that car, except that they have put faith in flashy displays.

A full head of elegantly coiffed hair is no guarantee of intelligence within. A sharply dressed man may be dull as a rock when it comes to what they understand of the world.

For us to know the true worth of something, we must look beyond the packaging. And this takes time.

Better that you sit with a single book and work your way through its pages, than to skim a hundred dust jackets and think you have gained wisdom from primary colors and blurbs.

Better that you engage in deep conversation, where you actively listen to your companion before you decide whether there is substance to their words.

And when you are building your own substance, do not look to the surface but look within. You are most productive when you attempt the least but do so thoroughly and completely.

Those who would judge you by your appearance are blind to your true value. The thing we should prize above all is invisible to a superficial inspection.

What is that, you ask? It is a well-ordered mind, working in harmony with circumstances and nature to bring about reason.

A person who can bring reason to bear in every situation is not led astray by emotions or bribery or threat of harm. They live content, untroubled by everything that plagues their fellow man.

Be well.

Chapter Nine

On Word Games and Worthy Matters

People spend their time in want and worry, and their earnest efforts are destined for futility because they are working towards ends that can never make them happy

You ask me to study your lengthy query, and I worry that your hand grew as weary as my eyes as you piled up the pages.

I shall be at leisure in my review, to give you a reply worthy of your own effort. Though I will not reply in kind, at least when counted in words. Rather, I will deliberate with care so that I may respond decisively.

In this I seek to be the good man that Confucius meant when he said:

> Does not the difficulty of deciding what is right
> to do necessarily imply slowness to speak?

And when it comes to what is right, let us remain a moment with Confucius to distinguish further:

> Better than one who knows what is right is one
> who is fond of what is right; and better than one
> who is fond of what is right is one who delights
> in what is right.

There are many who delight in wordplay, and they mistake their cleverness for wisdom. I am not overly fond of these, my dear reader, and neither should you be so easily amused.

When used to gain an unfair advantage over the unwary, words of influence are a stealthy tool in the hands of the adept.

But an audience brought to your side by trickery is like a nest built high in a swaying tree: It rests on an unstable platform and can be swayed again when the winds blow from another direction.

When your fragile point tumbles to earth, not only do you lose the high ground, but you have also given the crowd reason to question your own reason. Fool me once, shame on you. Fool me twice, shame on me.

"But," you say, "I am not talking about words used to convince, but rather to entertain."

If you spend any time with words, you will surely appreciate being brought to a smile by virtue of words being brought together. I think of the words from the Irish band U2 in their song *Running to Stand Still*:

> You've got to cry without weeping, talk without speaking, scream without raising your voice.

Although entertainment can be serious business, such word games are rarely the mark of a serious student. What they offer is but a distraction, and it is not harmless to distract yourself, let alone others.

The business of philosophy is to help man master reason, not to lose it.

People spend their time in want and worry, and their earnest efforts are destined for futility because they are working towards ends that can never make them happy.

- They want possessions, promotions, and power, and worry that what they have obtained will be taken from them.

- They are bothered by what others think, say, and do.

- They have time and waste it, good friends they take for granted, and have let luxuries deprive them of the enjoyment of simple pleasures.

- They turn a cold shoulder to the guests in their living room as they twitch the curtain aside in search of the ones they invited who do not arrive.

- Both responsibility and its absence torment them, and illness and death await, unbidden but unavoidable.

For all of these challenges, philosophy holds an answer. Shall we not dispense with play and get to the business of discerning what is right reason?

Knowing what is right, shall we not make sure that we climb down the ladder of our own desires to not only fondly consider the right path but to delight in leading the way?

You undermine both your case and yourself when you spend too much time in the company of word games.

It is not hurtful to tell the truth to those seeking wisdom; the real cruelty is keeping the truth to yourself for fear it will go unheeded.

And even though none hear your words, let your life serve as an example for any who are watching, now or later.

If you could wear a billboard about your person and stand in front of the doors of the bank, the car dealer, and the shopping mall, what words would you put upon it?

"It won't make you happy ..." deserves to be writ large on your front, and "The end is nigh!" upon your back.

Knowing that all things end, end your attachment to things, and you will find yourself on the path to happiness and nothing external can dislodge you.

Be well.

Chapter Ten

On Those Who Will Not See

Many people are the architects of their own misery, never realizing that with similar effort and much less worry, they could just as easily be about the building of a personal paradise

As if I needed yet another reminder that time is not one of the things given to humankind to control, I received your letter only today, though you mailed it many weeks ago.

- Was it COVID lockdowns that kept your missive locked in a dormant mailroom?

- Was it a canceled flight that kept your letter grounded and prevented it from flying to me with its usual dispatch?

- Or perhaps it was an overfull shipping container plugging the Suez Canal that kept your words from me, just as they kept shopfuls of sneakers and cheap cotton t-shirts from the shelves.

Although your words were missing in action for months, I trust that you have not been idle yourself but have been about the business of bettering yourself.

And what better way to do this than by remembering that the business of others troubling you is really just you causing trouble for yourself.

"What can you mean?" you say, "I am not causing others to behave the way they do. Should I now take credit for the sun setting and the moon rising?"

I would grant few people agency over their own actions, dear reader, let alone the actions of others.

No, what I refer to is how you respond to what happens, for this is the one thing that is always within your control.

Many people are the architects of their own misery, never realizing that with similar effort and much less worry, they could just as easily be about the building of a personal paradise.

What Plutarch wrote of Cicero in "The Parallel Lives" applies equally to many people today:

> He was prevented by many public affairs which were contrary to his wishes, and by many private troubles, most of which seem to have been of his own choosing.

ON THOSE WHO WILL NOT SEE

We can wish for what we have not and so make ourselves unhappy and choose to consume our particular poison and so make ourselves unwell.

But who says we can only wish for and choose that which makes us miserable and sick? I grant you full agency over your thoughts, my dear reader, and I urge you to see clearly and use your power wisely.

Seeing clearly is something that the ancient philosophers did surprisingly well when one considers that they had no benefit of corrective lenses, not to mention the corrective surgery, that we take for granted today.

Perfect eyesight is available to us today in the form of laser eye surgery, seamless bifocals, and daily disposable contact lenses. We are not to be without our prescription, be it in our sunglasses or in our specially formulated blue-phase shifting glasses designed for viewing computer screens.

If only our vision could be as clear as our eyesight.

For all of our 20–20 eyesight, I would say that we are more blind than ever to what is truly important.

- We run after riches, and we tell ourselves that we cannot get by on anything less. Then there are the pursuits we busy ourselves in.

- The farther you travel from the countryside, the less likely you are to find people who work with their hands.

- You may create virtual worlds in your coding and be transported to new heights on the backs of unicorns. But if you have lost thereby the simple pleasure of digging a furrow in the dirt, planting a seed, and nurturing it to flower and eventually fruit, you are less attached to the ways of the real world in a materially important way.

"Must I grow my own crops to be well fed," I hear you ask, "and travel about on horses shod by my own blackened hands to travel well?"

This is not my message.

If you would be satisfied with a day's labor, ask first if you have satisfied anyone's needs beyond your own, and then what harm you have wrought in bringing about your ends.

- Have you made people see and appreciate their lives more clearly by devising new methods to keep their faces planted to their screens?

- Have you made people see and understand their civic duties with more fidelity by rewriting history to suit a new narrative of systemic oppression?

- Does manipulating people to part with their money with the twaddle you call marketing bring into sharp relief that their happiness lies not in things, or are you throwing sand in their eyes?

"We are just giving people what they want," the professional classes cry. "And if we were not selling things of value, why are we being showered with money for our efforts?"

If there was ever a false indicator, it would be to follow the flow of money.

When you spend your day snuffing out one after another each of the faint lights that line the path to reason, do not then express wonder that all now wander aimlessly in the dark.

When with your distractions you poke a stick in the eye of mankind's ability to sit quietly in contemplation, I say you are no blindfolded judge of people's natural desire to see.

But though all voices are clamoring for our attention, and all hands are pushing us steadily away from our desired course, still we have it within our powers to see clearly.

Pull away the blinders from your eyes, for no one holds them to your head but yourself.

Free yourself of the burden of doing what others do just because they do it, and you become free to see the way back to the path of reason.

Be well.

Chapter Eleven

On Seven Popular Places

If you do not wish to be tempted, do not wander blithely through the bazaar of modern desires

Every place is the same as every other, dear reader, in the sense that we are all planted on the same earth, and the sun rises and sets equally on us all.

Why is it that some places seem destined to become places of wonder, whereas others bring out only the excesses in us?

I would have you avoid popular places altogether, at least until you have learned to tame your passions, for fear that in chasing what others call desirable you lose sight of what you should find valuable.

There are three types of modern-day meccas calling out the secular masses on their pilgrimages of tourism, adventurism, or debauchery.

For the tourist, consider the modern-day list of the seven wonders of the world:

- there is the Great Wall of China;

- the statue of Christ the Redeemer looking down from Corcovado mountain in Brazil;

- the Incan citadel of Machu Picchu in Peru;

- the Mayan ruins at Chichen Itza in Mexico;

- the Colosseum in Rome, Italy;

- the Taj Mahal in Agra, India; and

- the former capital of the Nabataean empire in Petra, Jordan.

Note that all but two of these are ruins, mute testament to great civilizations gone under. Most visit them to marvel at their accomplishments, though what we should be pondering are the reasons for their decline.

The grand adventurer is called to the great heights of the Seven Summits tour. To climb the tallest peak on each continent is to reach the penultimate height. Everest, Aconcagua, Denali, Kilimanjaro, Vinson, Elbrus.

"Penultimate height," you ask, "why what could be greater than this feat?" Remember that when it comes to one-upping our fellow man, humans display creativity unmatched by any less selfish pursuit.

ON SEVEN POPULAR PLACES

The seventh peak varies, you see, according to the explorer who lays claim to a new route to fame: Puncak Jaya, Kosciusko, Mont Blanc, Mauna Kea, Mount Wilhelm.

I do not doubt that some molehill is even now having its stature reconsidered if it will yield an alternative route to the Guinness Book of Records.

All these intrepid climbers are deemed mere amateurs, however, upon the addition of the North and South poles to the Explorer's Grand Slam.

I do not need to slam the lesson home for you, dear reader, to eschew the routes of both the "grand tour" tourist and the "grand slam" explorer.

You have a greater sense than that. But I sense you are showing a weakness for the third type of popular destination, and that is the party spot, one of the places people go to blow off steam and where we let human emotions run free.

These riotous pools of excess humanity are exemplified in the following seven ways:

- on Spring Break in Fort Lauderdale and South Beach in Florida;

- in the bars and beaches of Cancun, Mexico;

- among the beads tossed from balconies during Mardi Gras in New Orleans;

- anywhere in the clubs of Benidorm, Spain, or dotting the Levante and Poniente beaches;

- amidst the sweaty dancers of Carnival in Rio de

Janeiro, Brazil;

- behind the painted masks of the 72 hours of madness that is Dame Fasnacht in Basel; and
- ahead of the thundering hooves of the running of the bulls during the nine-day festival of Sanfermines in Pamplona, Spain.

What these all have in common is reckless abandon. The revelers give up their reason to bathe in emotion.

"For all the rest of the year that we are dutiful citizens, give me these few days to run free!"

If I wish to see people acting crazily, I do not need to see them drunken and heading for a night of unprotected sex. I do not need to hear them shouting and singing on their way to being hunched over a gutter spilling their guts in other noisy ways.

I can tell you without looking that their faces will be lined with dark circles and regret as they line up to board the charter flight back home to their "normal" life.

No, if I want to discern true madness, I will observe the office worker in their tower, the suburban parent about their errands, and the mall walker making their rounds.

Their "normal" lives are just as insane as when they are on holiday taking a "break" from their senses. Why is this?

Because they have set their whole lives in pursuit of things they know do not satisfy them or make them happy, and then they do it again and again expecting a different result.

For those who are training their minds, solitude may be the best way to avoid early unwelcome tests.

If you do not wish to be tempted, do not wander blithely through the bazaar of modern desires. If you struggle to tell what looks good from what will feel right, do not surrender your emotions to the passions of the ungoverned mob.

Better a single hour spent sitting in contemplation, cultivating your well-ordered mind, than a hundred hours lost to mindless revelry. How many hours do we spend in scrolling through TikTok videos or in never-ending games of Candy Crush?

We are so much more easily led astray than we are led forward, and once having left the path we find our way back only with difficulty.

It is not the places that lead us astray, dear reader, but our minds.

I would have you remember, though, that the places you are of a mind to go will shape your thinking, and may keep you from moving from the place you are in.

So heed my advice to avoid all places that allow you to avoid thinking, and you will think better of yourself for it.

Be well.

Chapter Twelve

On Philosophers, New and Old

Such is the bounty of philosophy: Though all are capable of being fed with what is already on offer, still we are ever creating new dishes to suit the palette of modern tastes

I am never so engaged with companions as when I am sitting by myself in my study.

When I am with friends, we converse about the topics of the day. These are the things that excite us and are designed to outrage us.

For the news is entertainment first and foremost, and information is secondary at best. Indeed, relevant information presented in context has the tendency to calm passions, not inflame them, so you will not find it often in today's media.

We talk of friends, absent and present. Your name came up, and talking of you gives me joy second only to being with you.

Much of the talk of friends is mundane. A promotion, an acquisition, a setback, a fall; parents moving from frailty to illness to death's door; children and their youthful mistakes.

Knowing what pitfalls lie ahead on the path is no safeguard against stumbling. It does not help a parent to tell their child such things, for some mistakes must be lived to be learned.

And, amidst the necessary lubrication that smooths all conversations, there is periodically a topic of worth and weight. But how few are the moments when such topics are safely raised.

If any are feeling stressed or unprepared, or if another has some news they wish to share, or if someone is distracted by a ping from their phone, the moment is gone, extinguished before it had a chance to flame into a meaningful exchange.

In my office, I have a most attentive audience.

They eagerly await my return, and I can almost hear them saying, "Finally! Someone has come to treat with our ideas."

Here there are no distractions I do not create myself, no interruptions I do not myself introduce, no superficialities to keep me from delving beneath the surface of things.

All the examples I need are on display before me:

- the good deeds I can revisit, and ponder the reasons why;
- the failures, faults, and blows of fortune I observe from a safe distance, and I need not offer condolences for

ON PHILOSOPHERS, NEW AND OLD

these deeds are also done and gone.

- I have nothing less than the condensed wisdom of the ages, the best from thousands of years and millions of people.

What kind of person would I be if I were unmoved in the presence of this multitude?

- Confucius and the Buddha, half a world apart, yet closer in spirit than many who live on neighboring streets.

- The Bible and the Quran, seemingly leading down opposite paths, yet treading the same ground more often than not.

- Plato and Aristotle, Seneca and Marcus Aurelius, each building on the solid foundations of the last.

- And I haven't even gotten to the contributions of the last two millennia, dear reader!

We each have the materials at hand to keep building the palace of human knowledge and wisdom.

Whether we are merely dusting off cobwebs in an existing great hall, rekindling light to shine again out freshly washed windows, or renovating a room that has fallen into disrepair from lack of use.

Some of us will go so far as to commence construction of an entirely new wing, for humanity is growing, and the many mouths need shelter and nourishment.

Such is the bounty of philosophy: Though all are capable of being fed with what is already on offer, still we are ever creating new dishes to suit the palette of modern tastes.

The goal of the meal is the same — to bring succor and feed life — but each generation is given the instructions to the printing press and encouraged to add to the book of recipes.

Though I may never leave the four corners of my study, I roam the halls of our human palace of wisdom freely and widely.

And where I find a window shuttered or a door blocked, and sometimes even a brick wall in my way, I am resolved to break through, pick up the rubble lying about, and keep on building.

Be well.

Chapter Thirteen

On Abiding in One Place

Progress is inversely proportional to the breadth of your focus. Include in your scope many things, and you will make little progress. Focus on one thing, and you will advance it the most

When I advise you to be steadfast in your thinking and your decisions, I urge you to abide in one place both physically and mentally. This does not mean that you make no progress.

"What can you mean?" you ask, "If I am bound to one spot, in my thinking, my abode, my actions, how am I making any progress? Life requires action, motion. I do not want to sit around doing nothing."

The answer is simple, dear reader, but also profound. I will give you several ways of looking at the solution, and you may choose the angle that suits you best. To start, let me ask you a few questions in turn.

- Do you think someone who drives their air-conditioned car 100 miles a day has learned more of the landscape than the person who walks daily the same quiet streets of their neighborhood?

- Does the politician who changes their mind hourly upon checking the prevailing wind of opinion have more profound thoughts by virtue of having had many conflicting thoughts?

- Is the person who purchases their weekly lottery tickets before returning home to their day trading more of an investor than the person who automatically directs a percentage of their income to an index fund and never thinks of it?

Just as the opposite of busyness is not idleness, busyness is no guarantee of productivity. How many busy people do we know who prodigiously waste their time?

When I say abide in one place, I mean three things: That you focus your efforts on one thing at a time, that you avoid distractions and temptations, and that you bend your will to making steady progress in a consistent direction.

In this way, you will move mountains. Continuous improvement is disarmingly powerful because it does not matter how slight the incremental steps are, just that you keep moving.

ON ABIDING IN ONE PLACE

Progress is inversely proportional to the breadth of your focus. Include in your scope many things, and you will make little progress. Focus on one thing, and you will advance it the most.

The reason we do not prioritize is because we fear the consequences of prioritization. To say "This is the most important thing I should be working on right now," is to say implicitly, "And everything else is less important."

Most people would rather drown themselves in work than admit that some things are more valuable than others. And though we know this is true, but do not act accordingly, what does this say about us?

Do not let yourself off the hook. Do the hard work of thinking about what is most important before you undertake any tasks, and you will have set yourself up for success.

Having set yourself up for success, shut the door to the many sneak thieves who would rob you of your progress. Distractions and temptations take many forms:

- Friends, gossip, the news, social media, TV and movies.

- Changing jobs, changing cities, vacations, travel.

- New information, more information, a better way.

- An urgent task, an emergency, a new priority.

I say barricade yourself in a fortress against the army fighting for your attention.

"You have gone mad," you say, "if you think the best course is for me to shut myself in a monk's cell and cut off all contact with friends, with information, with the real world."

If I am crazy, dear reader, it is for thinking that saying the truth will make people believe the truth. For I am telling you nothing but the truth here, though, of course, I exaggerate to make my point.

Yes, you need interaction with others, you need to pay attention to making your way in the material world, and you cannot stop time by putting your watch in a drawer.

But I urge you to consider that every moment you spend on something other than what you have decided is your most valuable pursuit is a theft you commit on yourself.

By no means do I expect you to work every hour of the day. No one is so disciplined, nor need be, although we can train ourselves to be more focused than we might at first believe.

The way to handle your rest, relaxation, and recovery is to make it something you actively plan and direct, rather than something that slips unbidden upon your consciousness and spirits it away.

When you take a break for exercise, when you meet up with friends for dinner, or when you leave your studies for a vacation, it will be because you decided it was the most important thing to be doing at that moment.

Give your rest and recovery the same priority that you would your work, and you will get the most benefit from it. Let yourself be pulled away from either your rest or work by giving in to distraction, and you are wasting your time in both cases.

ON ABIDING IN ONE PLACE

The last component, steady progress in a consistent direction, is easier to believe in after you have seen its effects for yourself. For now, trust me when I tell you that taking but a single step each day will bring you further along than all those whose efforts are heroic but sporadic.

You may still have days of mighty progress, and they will be welcome. But you should be just as happy to accomplish a tiny, incremental step, so long as it is self-directed and in the direction of your choosing. Because this means you are staying true to yourself, working on what you have decided is most important, and making progress.

I call upon American President Thomas Jefferson to reinforce today's lesson. His own actions were the proof of the truth of his words, judge for yourself:

> Determine never to be idle. No person will have occasion to complain of the want of time who never loses any. It is wonderful how much may be done if we are always doing.

Be well.

Chapter Fourteen

On Mind Viruses

The mind viruses are vices such as jealousy, greed, ambition, spite, and fear

So, I gather you think I have been rather informal in my emails of late, addressing weighty topics more like a casual encounter than a formal lecture with proper respect given to the subject at hand.

It is true that when I put my hands on the keyboard I imagine you are before me and we are simply talking. But do not mistake a comfortable conversation for one that lacks seriousness, dear reader. We are discussing important matters and their significance is not lessened though we try to keep our spirits light.

I do grant you that cleverness is no guarantee of correctness. In fact, the glib speaker who uses every oratorical trick is one whom you must attend to even more carefully. We are easily fooled by the surface of things, especially if they are pleasing to the eye, or in this case the ear.

Be especially wary of the hypocrite, the one whose actions in private do not match their flowery words in public. I work to achieve consistency of thoughts and deeds, and when I stray my wife is there to remind me.

I follow the dictates of my own thinking, and I am striving always to tell you what I think. If I also strive to string together my words in a pleasing fashion, let me do so in ways that shed light rather than merely dazzle.

We are always at risk of being dazzled because there are many things to distract us. A shiny new car, a sleek phone, and brightly-colored displays: These are specifically designed to entice us, and a great deal of thought and effort goes into making them appealing.

What then are we to think of the handsome and well-coiffed politician, promising to solve all our problems with other people's money and assuring us that nothing that happens to us is our fault?

- Is the politician also not an item on display, offered for sale to the buying public?
- And just how has he or she been designed to appeal to us? Is it to our better virtues or is the appeal to our fears and prejudices?

We are in a never-ending battle for our well-ordered minds, dear reader. For every hard-won step of progress we make in seeing through the surface of things to the substance beneath, a hundred new temptations and distractions are paraded before us.

ON MIND VIRUSES

It may help to think of your mind like a powerful computer, capable of performing the most amazing feats, but with this flaw: the input/output channels are hardwired to be completely unprotected against viruses.

Do you think you are safe because you have avoided being infected by such obvious conspiracies as QAnon, Bill Gates' plan to inject us all with microchips in vaccines, or the idea that the World Economic Forum is really a cover for the Illuminati seeking our subjugation via the so-called "global reset?"

I say take no comfort from the follies you have spotted. Say you have taken fifty steps safely in a minefield. Does that mean you should kick up your heels and run freely? If a sniper has fallen silent for a while, will you be the first to poke your head above the parapet?

And coming back to our computer, what would you think of the person who says "Oh, don't worry, I ran the anti-virus program two years ago when I set up my desktop?" You would back away from them slowly, just as you would an unexploded land mine because this person is a danger to themselves and others. That they are oblivious to their condition is sad, but no less dangerous.

This is your choice, dear reader: Either take regular steps to be on your constant guard or risk becoming a ticking time bomb of discontent, ready to explode at the slightest provocation of Fate not going your way. Once you realize that the mind is not immune from viruses that come in many forms, you will see the necessity and wisdom of running your personal anti-virus program daily.

"Tell me more about these viruses," you say, "and what is the protection program you speak of?"

The mind viruses are vices such as jealousy, greed, ambition, spite, and fear — all things that we know of and have been trying to put in their proper place. Just like a computer virus compels the CPU to perform destructive actions against its programming, so do mind viruses compel you to actions that erode your contentment and happiness.

Being infected with vices blinds us to the true value of things and causes us to pursue things of little or no value at the cost of our peace of mind.

Your protection is reason applied by the well-ordered mind. By checking every input and every stimulus against your pre-programmed list of personal values, you can identify when you are being offered a false good or false emotion.

Remember this: There are very few "trusted sources" in the world. Virtually all minds have been infected by bad ideas and sloppy thinking and thus their course of thought has been corrupted.

Though they may have the power of life and death over your person, do not give them unfettered access to your mind! It is the one place you can be secure in your self-possession, but only if you do not throw open the gates to any vandals who seek entry.

I do not mean to tell you to cut all connections to the world, tempting though that seems at times. We are social creatures, with moral responsibilities not just to ourselves, but to those close to us as well as to broader society.

Open the connection to let the world into your mind but filter it as carefully as you would drinking water from a muddy stream. Your connections to others bring you life's essence, but only so long as you do not poison yourself by consuming everything offered.

Be well.

Chapter Fifteen

On Popular Authors

By using your reading as a mirror into your own thoughts, you train yourself to pay attention to your mind

I have told you to spend your spare time in reading to train your mind. That you should read widely and well, sampling many authors across time.

That when you read, you should seek to make the lessons more than fleeting by taking them to yourself, for example by summarizing them in your own words. In time, you will be able to build your own new structures using the materials you have stored in your warehouse.

I may have left you with the impression that your leisure reading must be on weighty subjects by serious authors if you are to add value to your stores.

No doubt you gain from studying the greats, because these will give you strong foundations to build upon, steel girders that can hold the weight of the tallest towers. But remember that the materials abundant in most buildings are more common stuff:

Walls and ceilings made of drywall, concrete blocks, and bricks and mortar.

No matter whether you expect to learn the most from the masters, it is worth considering why the less serious topics and more popular authors have such reach.

Why do they sell books in such abundance, and how do they keep their readers eagerly clamoring for more? The academic dismisses these questions easily because they know that critical acclaim is no indication of correctness.

Indeed, the worst insult a certain type of scientist can levy on a colleague is that they are a mere popularizer of science, and not substantive in themselves.

But I ask you, what is wrong with making something understandable to many? Writing on complex topics in a manner that only a few can decipher is no great feat and not uncommon. It is a far greater task and eventual accomplishment to take a complex topic and make it understandable to all.

For the moment, let us ensure we are not ourselves snobs, but ready to take wisdom wherever we find it. Is there wisdom to be found in the best-seller list, and if so, why?

At this moment I expect you are calling to mind all the times I told you to avoid the self-help aisle like an active minefield. Though I gave you permission to sneak one or the other volume from these explosively dangerous shelves, am I now giving up my caution by opening the shopping cart to this year's summer read?

I think it is a mistake to dismiss Stephen King as no more than "America's schlockmeister," even though he himself says he is resigned to this fate, or to say that J.K. Rowling is not serious because she writes of wizards and magic.

Do we value less Elmore Leonard's gift just because he wrote crime fiction? Michael Lewis writes no fiction at all, but do we relegate him to the top of the display of "popular titles" because he writes individual vignettes tied loosely together rather than weaving tightly wound grand theories?

What do all these authors have in common?

- Stephen King delves into our deepest fears. What he finds there is not pleasant, but can anyone deny that it is a true reflection of what lies hidden within humankind?

- J.K. Rowling spins daydreams, fantasy, and wish fulfillment into epic tales shot through with darkness, suffering, and pain. This combination of the delightful with the spoiled, the pure with the soiled, is no less true than Stephen King's visions.

- Elmore Leonard had a gift for writing dialogue so true to life that you felt yourself a bystander in every scene. You feel less like you are reading an Elmore Leonard novel than living it alongside the characters.

- Michael Lewis's gift is to see the uniqueness in each individual and to let them speak in their own voice. By shining a spotlight on so many individual foibles and peccadillos, we have a chance to recognize ourselves in others.

The thread tying them all together is that they speak honestly and truly about the human condition and about our emotions:

What we long for, what we fear, and what makes us angry, sad, and happy.

You would think that because we all feel these emotions, it would be a trivial matter for an author to describe them honestly without omission or exaggeration. And yet it is rare.

Do I take away some of your enjoyment when I tell you to take a lesson from your reading?

I would say do not let me detract from such pleasant times, read and enjoy what you are reading. But if you would be a sincere student and not just idle away your hours without profit, then periodically stop and ask yourself why.

Why did you enjoy that last chapter so much, and why did that other disturb you? What was it exactly that transported you effortlessly from your couch to another world?

The answers to these questions will give you insights into the human condition, but even more so into your own condition.

Your own condition varies from day to day, though you may feel always like the same person. Has it ever happened that a book you loved suddenly turns odious and you find yourself loathe to pick it up, let alone finish it? Has the author turned treacherous, or is it you who has come into a different state of mind?

Both are possible, and you will know the truth if you are mindful in your reading.

By using your reading as a mirror into your own thoughts, you train yourself to pay attention to your mind. This helps form the conditions for following the reason of your well-ordered mind in other things.

In this way, your reading for pleasure will be no less useful to you than your most dutiful studies. If the latter teaches us what we should do, the former can help guide us in how to do it.

Be well.

Chapter Sixteen

On the Greatest Threat

You are never closer to danger than in the presence of your fellow humans. You are safer tucked away in contemplation of ancient wisdom

If you pay too much attention to the news, you will come away worried about all the wrong things.

- Will you be caught up in a twister, carried away by a flash flood, or struck by an errant bolt of lightning? And that's just from watching the weather channel.

- Other channels of doom will tell you to live in fear of dying from lead-poisoned water, radon-suffused earth, and second-hand smoke-filled air.

- Then there are the industrial accidents, derailed freight trains, and collapsing bridges you must assiduously avoid.

That such things happen is undeniable, dear reader. That they are rare indeed is never mentioned, and you could be forgiven for placing wrong odds on your chances of encountering misfortune in such a newsworthy manner.

We do not talk of the greatest danger to people, which is immeasurably more likely to rain down upon us than a piece of space debris falling from the sky.

"What is this great danger," you ask?

It is our fellow people.

You are never closer to danger than in the presence of your fellow humans. When provoked by the tiniest of slights we are something to behold.

And we do not need to be angry to be destructive. Our capacity to do capricious harm also knows no bounds.

- Did early settlers not shoot tens of millions of buffaloes to death out of nothing more than boredom, leaving carcasses to rot across the western plains?
- Carrier pigeons once flew in the billions across the summer sky, hurried now to their graves by the wanton destructiveness of humankind.

If we were better judges of the truly dangerous, we would free all the animals in the zoo and relegate the human visitors to locked cages for the safety of all.

You cannot eliminate your danger from this source, only reduce it.

ON THE GREATEST THREAT

Be aware that *any* provocation risks being too much, because it is viewed through the eyes of the recipient. You may think you are being amusing or that your insult was but a little thing. Murderous rage has sprung from a wayward glance, the corners of the mouth turning down at the wrong time, to say nothing of an actual encounter with someone prone to violence.

You are safer in the company of the dead, which is one reason I tell you to have your philosophy books about you in great numbers. When safely tucked away in contemplation of ancient wisdom you are less likely to give offense to the living.

However, you give offense even by your absence because we are annoyed by everyone who stands out.

"What, the world is not good enough for you that you feel it necessary to withdraw into seclusion?"

You will be misunderstood in the presence of your fellow person, and you will be misunderstood alone. But at least you make yourself less of a target when you quietly study, and that is something.

Be well.

Chapter Seventeen

On Treading Safely

Remember that being polite costs you nothing while being indifferent may cost you everything

I take it from your response that you think I was too pessimistic in my recent assessment of our fellow person.

"You have exaggerated once again the situation," you say. "Surely it is not so dangerous to be out among humankind."

I say that I have not been dire enough in my warning if you still doubt the point. I am deadly serious, dear reader, but my point was not to have you live in fear or live in seclusion.

Let me thus tell you how you can more safely co-exist in the world.

I told you that people are dangerous and now let's consider specifically what makes them dangerous. No doubt you will readily agree that much harm springs from the passionate emotions of others like envy, hatred, and fear.

Let me consider them in turn and arm you with your defensive weapons against them.

You do not need much for people to envy you. In fact, when you probe your own feelings, you will be forced to concede that the condition of envy is not brought about by abundance but merely by difference.

No matter how little a person has, you will be tempted by envy if they have more than you. No matter how much you have, if another has a penny more you will not rest easily.

The only way to avoid envy is to avoid scrutiny. If you flaunt your possessions do not expect adoring acclaim, only envy.

I do not ask you to become a hermit but give thought to your public displays. The less you show publicly and the more you can content yourself with private displays, the safer you will be among your fellows.

Hatred arises so much more easily than we think. It does not take a great provocation to create passionate hatred.

Why this should be so I do not know, but we can observe it readily enough.

- A driver cuts you off on the way to work, and in that moment, you are ready to abandon your commute, your respectable profession, and everything else.

- For a moment a grim fantasy plays through your head of following that driver to the ends of the earth so you can grind them to dust under your unforgiving boot.

- And then they raise a hand in acknowledgment that they momentarily inconvenienced you, and all is forgotten.

If a murderous fantasy can be called to life by something as trivial as a few seconds' delay in traffic, believe me when I tell you that to interact with people is to engender hatred.

At a minimum, do not deliberately provoke people. I say go a step further and be alert to potential inadvertent slights. Be quick to apologize for all things.

Remember that being polite costs you nothing while being indifferent may cost you everything.

You can use the words of that great counselor Seneca to guide you. The wise man

> will not misinterpret a word or a look; he makes light of all mishaps by interpreting them in a generous way. He does not remember an injury rather than a service.

Now comes fear. There is nothing we will pursue more avidly than attempting to crush out that which strikes fear in us.

Observe how one who fears spiders will crush their lives out and spray poison in copious quantities. The response is out of proportion to the threat, but it is the injury to our peace of mind that drives the overkill.

When you make someone afraid of you, they may appear subdued. But in their minds, you are a threat to their peaceful existence, and they cannot rest while you are a threat.

How do you avoid being feared? Do not avenge slights. Make light of them. Remember the Buddha's words:

> You throw thorns. Falling in my silence they become flowers.

Call to mind the sound advice of Epictetus:

> You will meekly bear a person who reviles you, for you will say upon every occasion, 'It seemed so to him.'

So far, I have been talking about the harm others can do to you, and how to arm yourself against these dangers. There is one danger greater than all this that I would have you avoid, and that is the danger you do to yourself.

I refer now to the failure to behave honestly and honorably in your actions. Bring to mind the Buddha's words here as well when he says:

> So long as an evil deed has not ripened, the fool thinks it is as sweet as honey. But when the evil deed ripens, the fool comes to grief.

Your misbehavior will arouse in others the emotions we have been discussing. But it will also give rise to painful emotions of your own. Doubt, shame, fear of exposure. All these are a steep price to pay for the temporary satisfaction of giving in to your base desires.

When you behave wrongly, the punishment of the state is but confirmation of the sentence you have already laid upon yourself.

So these are your instructions for how to make your way more safely in this world, dear reader. I sleep more easily knowing that you are well-armed for modern life.

Be well.

Chapter Eighteen

On Slogans

It is precisely when you find your emotions aroused by a small handful of words that you must force yourself to pause. Someone is almost certainly trying to manipulate your thinking for their own ends

You know I am no fan of sayings in philosophy. I object to them when they serve as a substitute for the hard work of thinking about and understanding underlying principles.

They have their place as reminders for the scholar and reinforcement for the student. But too often they take the place of thinking and are taken for the substance of an argument rather than merely the headline of an article.

Recently I was reminded of my distaste for superficialities in another context, politics. I sometimes reminisce on the happy hours I once spent reading a favorite newspaper. I am probably misremembering because really the media has done me a favor by becoming so blatantly partisan.

I now no longer have the slightest expectation of being objectively informed when I read a "news" story. I consider each article to be pure propaganda and the only question is whether the author made any attempt to hide their agenda.

I feel like the unsophisticated investor talking to the Wall Street banker: It is not a question of *whether* they are trying to screw me over, just a matter of *how* they are trying to do it this time.

I do not see any distinction in attempted persuasion between the opinion pages and the news section. In fact, I consider opinion writers to be the more intellectually honest. At least they openly purvey their views under an accurate banner.

The whole industry is moving to the realm of subjective opinion, though. Newspaper employees and pundits have largely dropped the pretense of objectivity altogether, whatever the header says above their byline.

There are some journalists who it appears have refused to pervert their writing to partisan ends or sell out their integrity for clicks. You will not find many working for major publications or on television. They have gone underground because the mob has declared open season on honest views, honestly stated.

Books are pulled from store shelves; electronic copies disappear not only from the online store but from your downloads as well. If there was ever an argument for paper copies of important books, it is that small-minded totalitarians have a harder time eliminating them from the world.

Book burnings serve to illuminate only the hatred on the faces of the zealots throwing volumes on the fire.

Where have these honest journalists found their havens? Where will you find them today, speaking out bravely against the unthinking erosion of all the progress humankind has achieved? On private servers and members-only sites that place barriers to public view. How ironic that the spread of free ideas today takes place in secret behind locked doors.

If you want to see examples of our much-diminished breed of free-thinkers, dear reader, here is where you can still find them: Look to Substack and Medium to find independent authors, Locals for communities of content from creators of all types, Rumble for videos that are not censored for political correctness, and X for unfiltered speech.

"I see the same developments as you do," you say "and I agree that it is tragic. But what does all this have to do with slogans, or have you forgotten the point?"

I have not forgotten the point, dear reader, although I thank you for keeping me from straying further. The reason philosophy fails to find more adherents in any age is that thinking is hard.

For the same reason that we ourselves find it tempting to give in to our vices, to let go of our discipline, to tell ourselves sweet lies: It is easier than accepting the hard truth that real progress requires hard work, in all arenas of life.

- If I want to be physically fit, I have to put in effort and make sacrifices. I need to pay attention to what I eat and plan tactically to expend my energy. I need to work on my fitness.

- If I want to advance in my career, I need to first let go of the daydreams of shortcuts and the resentment at unfair treatment I see all around me. I need to work at my job.

- If I want to be happy, I have to gain the upper hand on my otherwise untamed mind and bring its wild excesses within the control of reason. I have to work on maintaining reason.

All this is hard work, and there are limits to how much effort any person is willing or able to sustain. So we find ourselves relaxing, first in little things, and in just a few areas.

But see how our indulgences grow with the least of efforts! I had salad for lunch, so I could have a Big Mac for dinner. I parked a little farther out on the parking lot today, so I will take the elevator and avoid the unforgiving flights of stairs. I was at the office late last night, so I am playing a round of Angry Birds now.

These transgressions you can at least easily observe, for you see them with your own eyes. The indulgences we grant in our thinking are invisible but just as insidious. Because thinking is hard, and the conclusions can be painful, we devolve to slogans.

"At last," you say, "he is coming to the point!"

Be patient, dear reader, for I am trying to teach you a lesson as well in *how* I teach my lesson. I could have given you the point in a single paragraph, but would you have understood it as well without knowing the reasons why? Would it stick in your mind beyond the minute it took you to read it?

I would have you avoid the same trap of shallow thinking that is the result of consuming only sayings or slogans because they are an easy substitute for thinking. So, though it seems like I wear out your patience with my plodding, at least remember there is a method to my meandering.

ON SLOGANS

The examples in politics that brought me to this way of thinking come from all sides:

- Make America Great Again and America First *versus* Black Lives Matter and Antifa

- Defund the Police *versus* Law and Order

- Follow the Science *versus* Science Denier

Listening to what passes for public debate today, you could be forgiven for concluding that our attention span has diminished to encompass no more than three or four words.

And yet, could anything be clearer than the fact that a few words can move mountains? That passions can be inflamed by nothing more than fifteen or so letters, strung in a particular order?

Philosophers know better than most that ideas are powerful and can have an impact on the mind far out of proportion to the size of a sentence. Propagandists have learned this lesson all too well.

Moreover, propagandists are much cleverer than philosophers in expending their efforts. While we spend hours debating the substance behind our ideas, they content themselves with the catchy slogan.

They know the inherent laziness of people means they will be satisfied with the surface appearance. A few words impel the masses to action. The fact that there is but little substance beneath the surface is irrelevant because the crowd is already on the march!

I am not suggesting there is no substance behind the slogans I listed above. The reason the words are powerful is precisely because they touch on matters of great importance.

My complaint is that they are doing just that — touching the surface and relying on human laziness in thinking to do the rest.

Two people hearing the word "Antifa" will imagine very different things. The one will say, "I am against fascism, and Antifa means 'anti-fascism' so I must be in favor of Antifa."

The other will say, "Antifa members are behaving like anarchists. They protest violently, destroy property, and advocate the overthrow of government. I am against all those things, so I cannot be in favor of Antifa."

One person reading about a study that makes a conclusion that is to their liking (say drinking red wine and eating chocolate lowers the risk of heart attack), feels justified in their behavior and virtuous for "Following the Science." That the study was funded by the Alcohol and Cocoa Foundation, its results were taken out of context, and then misleadingly reported by a journalist who didn't bother to read the study is not important.

The nutritionist who tries to provide a broader perspective is labeled a "Science-Denier" because this is much easier than trying to nurture a nuanced understanding of an issue. (If you think I am being too trivial with my example, see what happens to your brain if you substitute the words "climate change and global warming" for "red wine and chocolate," and you will understand my approach.)

I would go so far as to say this: You cannot achieve a deep understanding of a substantive topic if you limit yourself to slogans.

It is precisely when you find your emotions aroused by a small handful of words that you must force yourself to pause.

Consider first that someone is almost certainly trying to manipulate your thinking for their own ends.

Will you be such an easy mark, a willing dupe? Not you. Force yourself away from following your gut response. Rather put in the effort to apply your reason. This will help inoculate you from the mind virus that is spreading via slogans.

One final word of caution, dear reader. Just because you may have vaccinated yourself against a particular virus in the form of a slogan, remember that the virus is still spreading wildly among the unprotected public. This is why you see competing slogans so often.

Propagandists on all sides are trying to infect the public first, not with the kind intention that we reach any kind of herd immunity, but to ensure that their ideas are the ones that take root in unsuspecting minds.

If you needed another reason to avoid social media and what passes for public discourse, this would be it.

Be well.

Chapter Nineteen

On Being a Nonconformist

The anarchist beats in all our chests, and it is only through the collective surrender of certain freedoms that we retain any freedom to pursue meaningful lives

Nonconformism is a phenomenon primarily of youth.

If it is a badge of honor to rail against the system in passionate youth, we call the person who carries it on into middle age a dropout, never-do-well, or malcontent. It is somehow embarrassing to be a forty-year-old hippie, never having seriously joined the fray but residing always on the frayed edges of society.

A small glimmer of hope remains. If the nonconformist maintains their attitude into old age, they can regain a certain respectability if for nothing more than their dogged consistency.

But at best this person is regarded as an eccentric or a curmudgeon.

Why do youth find nonconformism so attractive? For some, it is a reaction to the early adulthood realization that society is attempting to mold them. What they previously never questioned or unthinkingly took for benevolence they now see as little distinguished from brainwashing.

"You want me to do *what* for the rest of my life? And you want me to do it so I can go into debt to buy a house and a car, and continue building debt to raise children of my own and then send them into the maw of the same educational machine that molded you and me?

"That's what you have on offer? No thanks! Screw your hard work and sacrifice, and loyalty to a greedy corporation that has no loyalty to me. I think I'll travel the world instead."

There is a reason the Peter Pan story holds allure, dear reader. How lovely to think that we can stay children forever, never having to take up the world's cares.

Others go a bit deeper in their thinking, realizing that their childhood must one day end.

These individuals understand that they will assume burdens as adults and that societies perform useful functions in curbing humankind's worst excesses. They grasp that if we left everyone to their own unstructured devices, the result would be far from paradise.

But they do not accept the system at face value, first because they were given no choice in the matter (the brainwashing almost worked!) and second because the system has such obvious flaws.

They will ask, "How can any system so riddled with problems, injustice, and unfairness be the best way to proceed?"

This latter group has come further in their thinking, but they are still reacting to the surface of things and that is a dangerous place to stay.

It is a trivial thing to point out problems.

We must say to this group, "Sorry, my young friends, you will get no reward for finding the flaws abundantly distributed throughout life. In landing on the gaping cracks in the system, you have jumped over the much more important question: Why was the system established the way it was? What other systems were tried, and what was the outcome of those systems?"

I understand why youth lack humility because they also lack experience, which is a most able teacher. It takes multiple examples of the world not behaving as you confidently predict for you to begin to accept that you may not be perfect after all.

While I can forgive the confidence of youth, I do not forgive their ignorance. After all, the reason your ire is aroused is because you've realized you are in a system that is trying to shape you. In saying you will not be so easily duped, you have traded one set of blinders for another.

You say democracy is bad because it creates income inequality, and the rich appear to be getting richer. You say, because it seems a wonderous thought to you, that everyone would be better off if no one had more than anyone else, or at least if some wise person took wealth from those who have it and distributed it more fairly to those who lack it.

All fine. Here is what we say in return: "Before you step further in seeking to implement this change, do your homework. If you don't want society to think for you, think for yourself. How has this forced redistribution worked out in the societies that have tried it? Did you think you were the first one to have this idea?"

This line of thinking is most helpful to a large number of people and brings them back onto productive tracks in their lives.

- They realize that the collective efforts of millions of people over thousands of years have not just been random bumbling.

- They understand that despite obvious flaws in what we see around us, *if there were obvious fixes* we would have implemented them.

- They accept that sometimes a cure is worse than the disease and it is also possible to kill the patient.

A small number of nonconformists remain who are strong in their convictions. They know what they know — not only is the system corrupt but the people running it are corrupt. The system is not just flawed but broken.

And in what I find to be the most breathtaking leap, they believe they know how to fix it. With this group before me, I could forgive not just confidence but even ignorance if only they were not consumed with arrogance.

Especially when we consider that their "fix" requires first destroying our system so they can replace it with their new idea. And, finally, that they are the first humans in history to be without flaws, and hence they will not be corrupted by their new system.

Many calling for equality of outcomes are not looking for equality at all, but to upset the existing hierarchy.

ON BEING A NONCONFORMIST

- If others have power according to the current hierarchy, then let us tear this hierarchy down to the ground.

- We will reframe it in a picture more to our liking, in which the advantages you currently enjoy are taken away and given to us.

I suppose we are still talking of nonconformism, dear reader, but it seems the more descriptive word is anarchism.

With this last group, you can have no reasoned discussion or debate. Their purpose is not to learn, and certainly not to work within the established system. Their purpose is to uncreate, to destroy.

But nor can we simply wish them away.

No, the existence of this group of anarchists is the very reason societies came into being. We need civilization to tame our wild and destructive natures because they are dangerous if left unchecked.

The anarchist beats in all our chests, and it is only through the collective surrender of certain freedoms that we retain any freedom to pursue meaningful lives.

Let us not spend time wondering "Why are humans made so? What is it that makes us so dangerous to ourselves?"

We can more profitably answer the question "Discontent is a fundamental aspect of the human condition. What can we do to help avoid discontent becoming malcontent that leads to mass suicide?"

This is where philosophy's lessons hold their greatest promise. By teaching us humility and patience and instilling a desire to look beyond the surface of things.

And ultimately, teaching that conforming to our nature is not giving in to the bonds of servitude but opening the door to the happiness of a life well-lived.

Be well.